MW00989828

The poems in *Tintinnabu...*
places, though you could s...
the power of poetry, since the book explores how metaphor,
simile, imagery and sound can reveal connections that
are imaginative, revelatory and sometimes threatening.
Beveridge's creative use of language is most evident in the
section of the book titled 'Bizarre Bazaar' – where she plays
on lines and titles by Wallace Stevens (a fitting companion),
and offers linguistic elaborations on familiar objects, and
strange beliefs and customs. Each detail leads to others
through association, there is multiplicity everywhere, and
movement and energy, and this is as true of the poems
which capture the particular features of animals, the
transient effects of landscape, or the memories of people
and places, as it is of the language-oriented poems.

There is a range of styles, lyrical, dramatic and narrative,
which build on the achievements of poems in Beveridge's
previous collections. There is also an emotional range to
the poems: some poems are joyous, celebratory, ecstatic –
others humorous, elegiac, nostalgic – but the overall feeling
is of the joy and richness of language.

*Her luminous and sympathetic art brings us up close again
to the myriad creaturely realities equally important, clever,
emotional and wondrous as our own.* The Australian

*With joyous fluency and formal mastery, Beveridge...draws
the reader into an electrifying encounter with language,
guiding us through its flexure and torsion, its exacting grace.*
Prime Minister's Literary Awards

Also by Judith Beveridge

The Domesticity of Giraffes
Accidental Grace
Wolf Notes
Storm and Honey
Hook and Eye: a selection of poems
Devadatta's Poems
Sun Music: New and Selected Poems
Peregrine (chapbook)
How to Love Bats (chapbook)
Suddhodana (chapbook)

JUDITH BEVERIDGE

TINTINNABULUM

NEW POEMS

First published 2024
from the Writing and Society Research Centre
at Western Sydney University
by the Giramondo Publishing Company
PO Box 752
Artarmon NSW 1570 Australia
www.giramondopublishing.com

© Judith Beveridge 2024

Cover and design by Jenny Grigg
Typesetting by Andrew Davies
in 9/15 pt Tiempos Regular

Printed and bound by Pegasus Media & Logistics
Distributed in Australia by NewSouth Books

A catalogue record for this
book is available from the
National Library of Australia.

ISBN: 978-1-923106-05-5

All rights reserved.
No part of this publication may be
reproduced, stored in a retrieval
system or transmitted in any form or
by any means electronic, mechanical,
photocopying or otherwise without the
prior permission of the publisher.

9 8 7 6 5 4 3 2 1

The Giramondo Publishing Company acknowledges the support
of Western Sydney University in the implementation of its book
publishing program.

This project has been assisted by the Commonwealth Government
through Creative Australia, its arts funding and advisory body.

For Todd Turner

fellow traveller in 'the realms of gold'

Contents

1. Animals

Black-winged Butterfly

When I saw you as a caterpillar eating the vine's
new leaves, perhaps I should have flung you to the birds
but I didn't want there to be one butterfly
less to do the good work we need.
                    Finally, you've emerged—
but you can't untwist your wings, their scales
can't refract the light and raise your body heat.
Carefully I unlatch you from the edge of the chrysalis.
Against my fingers legs and feelers work in hard circles,
second-hands delirious for extra increments of time.
                    I offer you honey-water—
your proboscis, thin as a human hair, sips from my hand.
I think of how long you've spent in your sealed
bauble: the cocoon turning from green, to thin gold-leaf,
to black when the wings quickened. Now unable to open,
they're like the banners of a thwarted regime. Soon
you'll die in my palm, the only small holding you'll know.

Dead Possum

For days the possum's stink pulled the blowflies in—
they must have quit their garbage tips, their food dumps,
their compost, their public bins, their dog droppings
and other festering filth to spawn here and devil-sing.

I eased the carcass out from the slats in the gate—
then carried it away with a spade but the fly-pack followed,
a frenzied paparazzi, assembling and reassembling,
eager to make a maggot mass in the possum's flesh.

More and more came, thick and obdurate with a greenish
oil-slick glint and intoning feverishly like high voltage
as it bleeds from power cables, fervid satanic twanging,
demonic tremolos musing on damnation in the heat,

the cursed whines of old blues harmonicas doing time
at the cross-roads, anthems for an apocalypse in which
I foresaw thousands and thousands of maggots
creaming, risotto-like, inside my own half-eaten head.

Animals in Our Suburb, 1960s

Each kitten weighed no more than a sock. My father held
them down in the bucket, the water brimmed, and out of each
mouth came a cry and a small slew of bubbles. Weeks earlier
my mother had flushed down the toilet seven baby white mice
from a pair that would not stop breeding. Childhood seemed
to be a series of pets turning into pests. At night I'd hear

the local toms fighting, a sound of wild hissing—as if bagpipes
were asphyxiating. No one kept their cats inside. No one took
their animals to the vet. We found our cat, Tibbles, behind
a bush, dead with a suppurating eye socket. Every childhood
had a killing field: chickens running around without their heads,
drowned rabbits, drowned guinea pigs. A boy up the street

put a lit bunger into his cat's ear. Nearly every backyard
had its chained-up mongrel. Our neighbour kept an ex-factory
guard dog. It terrorised us with its bark, its hefty, grit-blasting
growl and weaponised face. It cut its teeth on cyclone wire
and trespassers. In our suburb no one had a lapdog. Who'd
ever heard of a Lhasa Apso, a Shih Tzu, or a Bichon Frisé?

Dogs were to ward off strangers, to eat the table scraps,
self-appointed avengers roaming streets with mange-ridden
skin, worms in their guts; bitches with hanging teats, or carrying
the new litter of ill-fated mutts—future puppies to be birthed
on a clump of newspapers or rags, licked into brute existence—
then dumped in an alley or behind someone's garden shed.

The Cuttlefish

When the fisherman sloshed the cuttlefish from a bucket
onto the cleaning table an alarm of pigments
                              flushed across its skin
then it discharged a cloud of greasy sepia ink
just before the man stuck a knife into it and its gills
                              leaked green blood.
He scooped out the glaucous eyes like galls
of plant tissue then held them
                              impaled on the tip of his blade.
The faint-pink bone he tore away floated like a tiny surfboard
              before it washed onto grey sand.
Pelicans ate the skin and entrails, gulls fought
                              over the eyeballs. Watching
I reeled, nauseated, as if the day had suddenly passed
                              through a light-splitting lens
changing everything into colour-coded horror.
Not once did the man look up from the steel of the table
              nor from his knives.
I looked towards the lighthouse, a gleaming, white pillar
of unsplit light orienting me back into ordinary daylight,
though I could still smell the blood's verdigris tang,
                              still see the displaced eyes—
the pupils dark, wavy: two tildes, two static ripples—
              pale fruit dripping from the end of a knife.

Vultures

High up, circling, they're miniature,
but quickly they spot a wound's aperture.
Ragged-out like sorcerers, with rowdy
style and bullying gait, they gorge
and glut—they'll even swallow bones
and teeth, help themselves to eyes,
noses and other birds' gizzard stones.
Yes, they rid us of stinking flesh—
but I can't stop my distress at the way
they savour the brains, the entrails
with equal relish, gorge on buttocks
and face with the selfsame appetite—
their rank indifference if the carcass
in the dirt is stallion, child, or rabid dog.

Mountain Goats

On slopes and ledges, on brinks and shelves, on towering peaks
of compacted snow, they leap-frolic
with more grace, poise
and perfected manoeuvres
than dressage horses on grass fields. They can pick their way
down a vertical bluff to reach a salt lick,
outrun cougars and wolves
like a chinook wind,
assess fissures with winged speed, scarcely halting to vault
over a ravine. When bears come,
or golden-shouldered eagles circle,
they bleat to warn
nursery groups at the watering holes. But when loud
cracks echo around the rimrock
of the high plateaux
or along cloud-shedding slopes
or around pedestals of ice-bitten rock—then every bleat
goes silent and every goat trembles
because it knows it will need
every sure-footed step,
sprightly leap and swift curvet, every triumph of brute
cunning over gravity to escape, not a rockslide
or avalanche—but hunters
whose stink arrives

on the thermals, hunters scoping them with bolt action
rifles, yearning to turn
their rock wizardry
into a loose skid,
a bone-breaking tumble to the bottom of an incline.
Hunters ready to wield knives,
saw off horns and hoofs
and call killing harvesting.

The Dancing Elephant

Although she was moribund
she started to sway her trunk and move
from side to side in a rotund dance.
She swayed like an iron bell
and I, too, started to sway, rolling
my weight as though I rode
the swell of her back, the swell
of her gait. Who could say
what led her to dance, to lean
into the light, to move the grief
her limbs held and drum a rhythm
of passing age, of ending breath.
Who could say why her dance
kept on, an hour or more, or why
I keeled, canted, not wanting
her dance to stop though the cold
climbed up my legs and rain
streamed down in grey sheets.
She barely blinked or moved her eyes.
She focused on the shuffling
of her feet. Her dark weight,
her slow carriage comforted me:
it was lunar, a manoeuvre
against gravity. I didn't know
if she saw me conducting myself
in her sway, her partner
in this geo-strategy of goodbye.

Then she stopped, turned in a circle,
staggered, shivered as though
she felt some command sharp
as a bull hook. She shook
like a theatre marquee nearing
collapse. My old charge, who'd
learned to solve the impossible
equation of her weight and balance
one-legged on a pedestal, to lift
herself on her hind legs as if
she were made entirely of cloud.
Was this why she danced, to show
me her incalculable pain, what
her muscles and bones had endured,
years in those chains, to show
how she danced for death
as she had danced for me? Yes—
I knew it—my cruelty. I'd goaded,
starved and whipped her until
broken, she became my spry,
spry dancer, my ballerina turning
and lifting her feet in the ring...
She flapped her ears, shuddered
once more... There was barely
any sound as she fell—just a small
insinuation of applause from the rain.

Dog, Old Jetty

I've come to walk along the jetty, watch the stingrays
glide around the pylons, their sides fanning and flaring
like the skirts of Spanish dancers, but there's a large dog
tethered to a pole, idling on low growl, speed-smelling
the wind. Perhaps the owner is at the other end of the bay
where the shore's spiked with fishing rods, the water
tented with sails, a new encampment of pleasure seekers
at the marina and resort. The wind is cold and whines
like a cowering animal. On the sand boats are breaking
down to their components like beached sea mammals.
There's a diesel spill in the shallows, rust on the hulls
like old blood. I speak gently but the dog growls louder,
a deep-throated rumbling—a Harley with the mufflers
removed. It pulls on its leash, barks as if it's received
a boot-driven command, an abrupt reminder of duty and rank.
I count the knots in its short stiff rope, hear as it moves
its nails click on the boards like ill-fitting keys. I see that
the spikes on its collar are as large as its teeth. Suddenly
a wave crashes onto the jetty, the dog shakes, twists
as if trying to remove a drenched overcoat, water flying
sharply off its back. I slip quietly past, walk to the jetty's end.
The dog, tail in broken wag, surveys the lonely horizon.

Bluebottles

So many swimmers ran out of the sea, branded with welts,
or wearing scarlet copies of the tentacles of a swarm of bluebottles.
They limped, yelled, rubbed sand, or poured water on the stingers,
and some, unsure of the correct first aid, applied ice cream,
even sunscreen, anything at hand: soft drink, hot coffee—

and some already sunburned, felt the stingers like a further
blowtorch, a raw franking, a due payment of blisters.
On the sand the bluebottles looked like air-filled dumplings,
tight balloons of nothing, soap bubbles on top of small bags
of laundry bluing. Kids with sticks lifted the tentacles

high then flung them to make strange patterns on the sand.
Some slapped the bulbous floats with their thongs, making
the sound of corks fired from popguns. I've never held
to divine supplication, never worn charms, crosses, or lucky
pieces, but that day I whispered a prayer that no tentacles

clothe me in pitiless scarlet, that no barbs pierce my body
with the lightning-quick, punching power of tattoo needles,
that I don't run out of the sea with my skin turning into
flocked wallpaper, my arms bearing a mock-up of my veins,
and my legs a sea creature's long hieroglyphs for pain.

Horses, Turon River

Six horses lean into one another. They snort, shake their manes.
They're stalled by the fence, a jerry-built dilapidation.

The river rears over stones, bucks against the banks,
fast flowing, free roaming, refusing to be broken in.

The horses huddle under lightning's stockwhips, under tiered
clouds: a grandstand of dark akubras, mist swirling like dust

in a ring. The river rushes onwards. The horses snort again
leaning their heads into the tightening bridles of the rain.

The Leech

You're a sycophant, repugnant. Vile bacchant—
you suck and glut, fill like a slimy phial. No denial
of the claret in our veins. Fat phlebotomist,
yes, you were used to treat ailments—fevers, gout,
haemorrhoids, headaches, clots, bleeding wounds
and gums—you thrived, made doctors rich.
            Gatherers, poverty-stricken women
wading in bogs and swamps found you with their
feet and legs. You'd cling on, swell like lustful phalluses
before dropping off; the women whey-faced,
ghostly, bled for many hours. Then your celebrity
as a cure-all changed and you lost your plentiful feasts.
            Tick, mosquito, louse, flea
or bed bug are not in your class, you with your
three jaws, three hundred teeth, your blood-thinning
spit. O adherent parasite, varicose hermaphrodite,
I've watched you cover my toes, black as gangrene.
No animal or orifice is off limits, you love a groin,
a bladder, the soft tissue inside an elephant's trunk.

Listening to Cicadas

Thousands of soda chargers detonating simultaneously
at the one party
*

The sonic equivalent of the smell of cheese fermented
in the stomach of a slaughtered goat
*

The otic equivalent of downing eight glasses
of caffeinated alcohol
*

Temperature: the cicada's sound-editing software
*

At noon, treefuls of noise: jarring, blurred, magnified—
sound being pixelated
*

The audio equivalent of flash photography and strobe lighting
hitting disco balls and mirror walls
*

The sound of cellophane being crumpled in the hands
of sixteen thousand four-year-olds
*

All the accumulated cases of tinnitus suffered
by fans of AC/DC, Motörhead and Pearl Jam
*

Microphone feedback overlaid with the robotic fluctuations
of acid trance music
*

The stultifying equivalent of listening to the full chemical name for the human protein *titin* which consists of 189,819 letters and takes three-and-a-half hours to pronounce

*

A feeling as if your ear drums had expanded into the percussing surfaces of fifty-nine metallic wobble boards

*

The sonic equivalent of ant juice

*

Days of summer: an auricular treadwheel

2. Walking with the Poet

Surfers, High Seas, Manly Beach

Surfers in wetsuits, tight as inner-tubes, watch the swell build—
most keep behind the breakers in chop that's a slough
of fuming white feathers. A gale blores through the Norfolk pines

shearing off branches, gulls holster their wings, litter scatters:
a salvo of missiles—and though spray blows in scurfy drifts
and sand pricks our legs in swift dispatches, though the cliffs

are blotted out in tissue-paper air, and each wave breaking
is as loud as a heavy-haul trailer blowing its tyres, we can't look
away from those few surfers who rise high on their boards—

platforms of pride, podiums of prestige—their arms held
out with the poise and sureness of wings, knees half bent,
braced, steadfast, ready to descend those baritone cascades.

Hawkesbury

i.m. Robert Adamson

Above the cliff a Brahminy kite circles on an updraught,
holds the scene in the keen, yellow charge of its eyes.
Earlier I watched a sea eagle ride a disc of air—
then suddenly pull its wings into a deft stoop,

a high-speed dive before it let down its talons like a set
of stevedoring hooks, snatching up a rat lying
in a warm coil of rope on the dock. Perhaps the kite
will take a fish from the water, or another nesting rat.

Now it simply circles, a slow enchantment whose purpose
seems impossible from so very high up. And you are gone,
Robert, from your high place above the water, gone
from the mudflats and the river where your words

conjured a raptor's view, the Hawkesbury surveyed
with your rapturous eye. I walk back to the wharf,
a crow calls with a voice of charred gloom. The kite
has drifted away to circle and hunt elsewhere. I watch

crabs on the mudflats work their claws around
mangrove roots pegged out like snorkellers. And I think
of you, Robert, pen in hand, breathing easily—words
angling deeply—poem after poem pulled from the river.

At Barrack Point

for Phillip

Today the weather is blustery, the chop is a ruckus of plucked feathers,
so many waves on white-knuckle rides to the shore. Surfers tumble,
their boards scutter upwards, backwards, shoreward—then they're hit
by another avalanching weight, a congested torsion of water that pounds
into the cliff, sprays up like a flock of startled gulls. Do you remember
the first time we were here, when you stood by yourself at the edge?
You wanted to feel with your toes the tide's drag, the moon's gravid haul.

Then we sat on the sand, you were mesmerised by the flow of waves
as if a magician were pulling endless scarves from a sleeve. Now I see
a boy, five or six, arms aloft, rock hopping. Startled, his mother calls,
telling him to watch his footing but her voice is lost among the dubstep
of the surf. He tires, comes down from the rocks and I can sense
the sweetness of their held hands. Now he steps on a cluster of cunjevoi,
each expulsion of water as amusing to him as the prank flatulence

from a whoopee cushion. In three days it will be your 27th birthday
and still I want to tell you to be careful, that disaster can be a loose stone,
a rickety stair, but your days are beyond my charge now. I can only watch
you go into the tumble of time, into the tidal bore of fate that can work
behind our backs to deliver setbacks, mishaps, who knows what adversity:
a wave generated elsewhere but reaching us eventually, no matter
whose hand we hold, how careful we are, no matter where we stand.

A Woman of Flowers

There's my mother in her garden, the bushes are pruned,
the edges of the grass trimmed. She takes a trowel, spreads
mulch over the dark soil, throws a grub to a waiting currawong.

A sprinkler bunts out long silver lines over pots, shrubs,
and newly planted seedlings. She rakes the leaves from the grass,
trims another hedge, ties a climber more securely to the trellis.

But now, at 96, she can no longer garden. She lies in ungodly
sleep, or just listens to the second hand's passage through another
endless afternoon. I wonder if she remembers the days

when, with secateurs in hand, she'd snip piles of clippings
into tiny pieces for the bin, or with scissors trim to an exact
measure the rough edges of the grass. Does she remember

the pollen-smitten insects in shifting illuminations
of morning sun, the passersby who'd stop to talk and tell her
how her garden brought them such delight? Her mind has lost

all *jouissance*—still I try slipping the past in, snippets where
joy might root, leaf and bud again, old memories that might
allow her to see all those days she filled with mothering honey.

To a Garland-maker

It must be good to be a garland-maker—
your daughters carrying water, working with you,
braiding feathers, shells, leaves, repeating the holy names
as they wreathe their fingers around the stems.

Daughters who never let the flowers fall to earth,
or bruise the petals. Daughters festooning doorways,
garnishing gateways, prinking up the palisades.
Daughters whose absolute bliss is marrying

themselves to this—baskets at their hips,
plucking flowers, licking threads. Daughters
who will adorn you at your funeral with blossoms
picked at dawn. It must be fine to be

a garland-maker—your daughters working
with you, weaving prayers around leaves, peduncles;
their breath as fresh as jasmine, meadow grass,
sprays of lavender on an evening breeze.

Two Houses

for Stephen

I found a rental with tall trees just beyond the back fence.
It was peaceful except for the three a.m. Friday freight train
slowly pulling the weight of its wagons along the tracks,
wheels grinding, couplings shrieking, derailing our sleep
for at least that six minutes of a much longer run
to get the goods into Sydney. Wherever it had come
from—Brisbane, Casino—that train would have travelled
through the night, a two-kilometre chain rattling
sleepers awake, but we didn't mind so much because
often at that hour, we'd hear the powerful owls
close by in the trees and we'd get up, take the torch
and wait for the light to show in their eyes, red beacons
flashing on and off like lighthouses if they blinked.
They were so close we could see the mottling and barring
of their feathers, layers of white and grey highlighted
with brown and charcoal chevrons, strong claws
gripping a branch. We'd listen for the slow, deep soundings
of the male, then the higher pitched call of the female,
a short catechism resolving territory and distance.
We watched at dusk, too, for their flight—soundless
distillations of moonlight in the shadows and the trees.
There were flocks of cockatoos also, like that freight
train shrieking us awake, taking us out into the timbered
dawn, our new haunt of astonishment. Everything
that year was new: your move from interstate, my shunting
an unsalvageable marriage to its dead-end siding, the gambit
we took in changing our lives. I've heard powerful owls

26

are the only birds that can carry more than their own
weight. No wonder they became our talismans. Once
we saw a mother owl feeding three juveniles, tearing shreds
from a dead possum. We'd find possums in the reserve
neatly eviscerated, the kills always silent... We live
elsewhere now, our own place. Sometimes, still, we hear
an owl, a male's wooing, and territory-declaring to bring
a mate in close. But we've only seen an owl once,
when sitting out in our yard, it alighted on a low branch,
its pearl-ash and dusty-grey feathers made it look like a puff
of fog against the apricot blush of dusk. Watching the owl
again I thought of how far we'd come—all the actions,
workings, means, and mechanisms across time and distance
to pull to its destinations this rich consignment of love.

Watching the Potters

How good to bring clay out of the ground
and into the sun, and as your hands girdle and caress,
to watch each clod rise to new worth—a pitcher
for water, a cup for wine, a jug, an urn, a lidded dish.

I would like to sit on the sun-kilned earth
and turn a stone wheel, build a column, arrest
a shape, a form, effloresce a rim or lip.
I would take my time, work without worry,

away from words, away from the slush
and slurry of human affairs. I'd smell the wealth
of the earth, its salts and ores, find profit
and plenitude in my wide-girthed pots, find joy

in cradling raw earth, soft and damp, slippery
as a newborn before I'd shape it, set its purpose:
a pitcher for water, a cup for wine, a jug, an urn,
a lidded dish, each cold clod fired to new worth.

The Breakwall

A few crabs are packed in the crevices of the breakwall,
tiny, flat landmines the herons and oystercatchers
are decommissioning with their bills. Earlier we watched
soldier crabs walk the sand like a bright-blue eyeball brigade.
Now it's nearly dusk, light is playing on a spill of diesel
that has the colours and sheen of liquefied opal.
You call my attention to an octopus small and flexible
as a ballet slipper in the shallow water under the wharf.
It senses us, turns bright red before taking on the grainy
texture of a rock. I do not yet know how often this memory
will recur, nor the image of the sea eagle suddenly dropping
from an air current as if every hold could be released
as easily as a slipknot. I do not yet know that the cormorant
on a pylon hanging out its wings, standing perfectly still
as if practising for a life behind museum glass, mounted,
stuffed, locked in an eternal vacuum, will become
another symbol of your absence. I watch a pelican's long
fricative skim while you walk ahead along the boards
to where some youths are fishing, their reels, as they wind
in their lines, clatter like coins on a table rattling out of their spin.
You're lost for a while to the distance where the jetty ends,
misted by spray. Sharp-mouthed gulls fly in, noisy, keen,
insistent, bargaining for something along the seawall.
We do not yet know that this is where we'll scatter your ashes,
disperse them across the harbour to float into the ocean
like handfuls of oyster grit, the pale leavings of seabirds.

Walking With the Poet

We came to the jetty at dusk. Jellyfish had washed
in on the tide and glinted like lenses from divers' flashlights.
When we saw the pelicans lumbering along the shore
you said they looked as if they were wearing galoshes
full of rocks. I commented on the spandex stretch
of their bills, their wings an elbowing jostle
when fishermen threw scraps. No words or analogies
can bring you back, but I summon a description
you might have made of these fishermen vigorously
winding in their reels: the clacking of flamenco heels
across a hard wooden floor. It's dusk now and lightning
scrawls its florid signature halfway down the coast.
A jellyfish, purple and grotesque floats under the pier—
an aquatic mushroom cloud, or a Spanish onion
rotting from the bottom up. I walk along the shore,
pick up shells—some fluted, some pinked at the edges,
some like brittle obsidian chips but tintinnabular
as trinkets when the small waves wash in. There's
a chinking of barnacles in the cracks of the pylons,
oyster shells spackled to rocks. That day walking
to the pier, we saw a brush turkey making a mound—
was it you or me who said its yellow wattle looked
like a collar of cold omelette? Another jellyfish rises
on the tide, a rice paper dumpling, you might have said,
the glint of the setting sun detonating in your eye.

Washerwomen at the River

holy Ganges, Rishikesh

No cloth too little for them to rinse, no stain or stench
too large for them to wring away with their small,
hennaed hands. They make a rhythm dashing cloth
on rock: a thump and a tinkling counterpoint—

their bracelets' glassy spills. I listen to them carry
laughter to their labour like full pitchers—they sing,
they quip, they work in lissom rhythm loosening
dirt, slapping away our loudest and our quietest stains,

our most extravagant and our most mundane.
The days flow by like sunlit treacle and we give
them more to wash, a never-ending sequel to our
stories of blood, sweat, muck. Even the air seems

cleansed by starry explosions of water on rock.
I praise them at their rounds, beating cloth on rock,
freeing us of our guilt, the soiled exposure of our
limbs and loins, all the errands of our careless hands.

The Waitress

After her shift, as she walks home under the streetlights
perhaps she'll see that stars have filled the sky
like change in a tip-jar, or remember how out on the bay
in bright sunshine, windsurfers steered sails
like huge cicada wings and clouds billowed above the office blocks
like rows of chefs' toques. Or perhaps nothing today
will defray her mood and she'll think only of the train
clucking across the bridge, how as she turned to watch
she felt a tightness in her neck, an ache in her shoulders.
Perhaps like the night before, unable to sleep and bitter
about everything, she'll sit with her knees up, arms
folded tightly around them, repeatedly turning her thoughts
like pages of a stale menu. Now she lingers along the pier.
A cruise ship vast as a glacier glints at the terminus.
Passengers with dreams as brightly labelled as their luggage
pack the gangway. Perhaps she could find a job on one—
a croupier, cocktail waitress, spa hostess, see Fiji, Tahiti,
Honolulu—she's always loved the breezy sway of that name.
She blows away her dream with a smoke ring, knowing
she's spent too long on the pier, that she should be
taking orders, wiping tables, jostling cutlery and cups.
She walks past the souvenir shops averting her gaze
from her reflection. The restaurant door swings open
to table chatter, piped music, wheezing coffee machines.
The manager leers at her again and she wonders if her
future will always be bar-coded to someone else's price.
She clears a table, exchanges a few words with a woman

who swipes a card then drops a coin into a bowl.
The bar is noisy. The kitchen a cacophony of dropped
crockery, the chef's steel-edged voice yelling
that the desserts for tables 9, 11 and 15 are still awaiting
pick-up. From a window she can make out the prow
of the cruise ship— an enormous wedge of white cake,
silver lights glinting like nonpareils. *Honolulu* she whispers
to herself again as she carries the desserts to their tables
her legs wobbling as if she were on the deck of a ship.

Two Brothers

Bibo and Jakov lived with six cats in their green fibro house.
The two brothers worked on the docks—they always said
'stevedoring'—refused to be called wharfies or dockers.

I could hear chains clanking, a sea wind blowing through
an open hatch, tools cutting through metal as they spoke
about their waterside lives, the cats winding through

their legs like smoky veils, sometimes sunning on the porch,
paws lazily palping at mice in their dreams. At knock-off
the brothers came straight home to tend the garden

and feed the cats. They'd often give my mother potted herbs,
plates of pastries stuffed with cashews and dates, boiled
apples filled with walnuts. They'd give me glasses of spiced

milk and let me play with their cats while they took showers
to wash away the insults, mostly from labourers with fists
the size of blacksmiths' hammers, tattoos flowing down

their arms like an outer network of veins, profanities about
disputes, scabs, and immigrants steaming off their tongues
as they clustered around the pubs like drain flies after work.

One late afternoon we heard Bibo and Jakov out on the porch,
their voices explosive with anger and grief. Five cats: Nada, Jamina,
Enas, Feriz and Malika, named after family members killed

in Sarajevo, were hanging by their tails from the clothesline,
drowned. It was someone's cruelty—perhaps a neighbour,
or one of the dockers who didn't like the garlic, bean soup,

or stuffed peppers on their breath, or the language they used
to express a longing for spruce and birch forests, the scent
of orange bellflowers, the taste of bramble gin, the calls

of the marsh tit, the river warbler, and nuthatches that build
mud nests and climb down trees head-first...those cats
swinging on the line, dripping like old black grease cloths.

At Flying Fox Bay

I took a portion of mineral and bone grit from the urn
        just before your parents finished spreading
your ashes around the base of the fig tree. Now I've come

to return what I've kept for sixteen years. Touched often,
        the cache became a powdery pebble dash,
something I'd press my fingers into whenever grief would

grind its grist. The tree seems smaller than I remember,
        new walkways, playgrounds, and barbecues
have turned your childhood haunt into a much-visited site.

I think of you climbing trees, looking out at the shoreline,
        onto the water, a hidden cove of light-hoarding,
light-gathering gold. Now, I put grief's particles

onto the sand at the tree's base, this once outlying place
        where you'd roam, play, invent the best
games so that all the kids sought you out to make

their time here wild, inspired, better than any television.
        You knew the dark, overgrown hideouts
that lead to the most fun. You knew what role to give

each sun-brown, hellcat kid so that they would go
        along with you like alter egos, those days when
the only play equipment was the bush, the water,

a flying imagination, and a strong climbing-hold.
    Perhaps I shouldn't have taken that pinch of you,
but I needed something solid, an intimacy I could touch.

Now that the grains have left my hands, my fingers
    will no longer read grief's repeated specks, but
I'll come here—often—and dig my fingers in the sand.

3. The Bizarre Bazaar

Moon Poem

You're a spoonful of curds and your falling light the whey

*

You're a squirt of milk from a sow's udder

*

Friend to the wolf and owl but your true alliances
are to the snails and silverfish that eat fishermen's almanacs

*

You are not musical but you're rhythmical

*

You're the snow-blind eye on frost-bitten space

*

You're the line of face paint under the bottom lip of a clown

*

You're a plague sore on darkness

*

You're a decentralised currency, bit coin that evades human teeth

*

You love flowers that night-bloom
and children and old people who befriend their inner lunatic

*

You have deep facial divots—perhaps you were the inspiration
for Elizabeth I to spackle her cratered skin

*

You're a private secretary in a whitewashing officialdom

*

In waterways you're a smear of milky broth, in doorways
and bedrooms you linger like the smell of smoke

*

Two nights a month you're the venom-tooth of a snake

*

You're a pill in a blister pack of cloud

*

You're every ocean's private disco ball

*

If you could write a book, it might be called *Fool Moon and Other Lunacies*

*

You're the heartland of Witch School

*

You're an apparition widowed to an unborn ghost

42

Incense

The merchant told me this scent will drive away
trouble and despair and purify the base instincts.
He drew it slowly under his nose, said it was made
from Himalayan poppy, that its oil was difficult
to extract, impossible to imitate, but when lit
would provide me with all I needed to know about
grace and ardent desire. He took another stick—
told me its scent was made from buds that blossomed
after dark, under the influence of a spotted nightjar
calling only during a new moon. Mixed with musk
it will stimulate kindness, infused with linalool
or aloe it will induce prophetic dreaming, if added
to saffron and the pulverised wood of a Persian oud
it will link the mind to insight and maintain serenity
in the home. I asked if he had a scent that could help
me interpret the throbbing sensations in my right
eye and left leg and increase patience and calm.
He asked my zodiac sign then suggested a blend
of jasmine, pine, cinnamon, and myrrh which must
be burned at dawn while I wear a ring of fire opal
and carry a handkerchief with an embroidered phoenix.
Later, as smoke rose from my rooms I detected only
ground fungus, goat dung, the singed wool of a dead ram.
I cursed the seller who'd duped me, but he was right
about one thing, just as he said, the smell lived on.

A King Sends a Delegation to Meet a Clan from the South

We've heard they make music
by tying copper pots to donkeys, tugging on the ropes
then beating them with wooden poles. We've heard
      their highest cultural achievement
is a poetry that never veers from the subject
of spitting in public places, that they torture

      hermetic dreamers
and anyone who perceives a Great Chariot among
the stellar immensities. Can it really be true
      they believe alliances
are jealousies, that they call the ongoing hum of things
a disease of the ear and recommend breath-holding

      as a cure? It's said they sing
hymns to a coterie of aged geese and at weddings
give gifts of broken cups, dented basins, torn robes
      and the clothes of the dead.
We've heard they have embassies underground,
that they're gathering information on clans

      from the north, spreading
rumours we choose our leaders from those who can
best predict the future from the scratching behaviour
      of flea-ridden dogs—
we can only think this is a result of their indulgence
in rancid goat butter and their belief that the mind

and the world are just shadowy
inventions and that wasps are lords of the sky.
I've sent a delegation carrying gifts of ivory, perfume,
        jewellery, pottery, leather
and copperware to show that our artisans are the most
delicately skilled. Our musicians will astound

        them with their rhythms and flutes,
and I have written a poem about mathematics
and its relationship to floods and plagues
        which I hope can be translated
and recited, though we've heard their language
lacks complexity and rigour, making it impossible

        to pursue perfection in thought.
Perhaps our sweetmeats can tempt them into trade
though we've heard they produce nothing of value
        except a liquor made from
cinnamon and snake venom. We'll offer them
our koumis, at a price of course, though we've

        heard their currency is puddle water
that spills and scatters like coins conjured in dreams.
I just hope they don't serve my hapless diplomats
        their notorious cuisine—fried
horse eyes and braised camel tongues in a thick
brown paste of their own fermented viscera.

Learning the Piano

I'm sick of scales   of trundling them out
forget this slow tempo   this Sisyphus work
I want my right hand to bounce   my left
to stride   I'm tired of the up and down
humdrum   of these strait-laced notes
a beetle with a dung ball   up the same path

I want sugar-plum swing   tutti-frutti trills
a roulade, a glissando   a big hunk of funk
instead of hands   sticky with impatience
thick with mistakes   I wish my fingers knew
where to spread   how to whip up from this
slew of notes   a few catchy bars of the jellybean rag

Ethical Reversals

Power plant	Plant power
Forbid	Bid for
Back hand	Hand back
Hold up	Uphold
Bystander	Stand by her
Travel time	Time travel
Farewell	Welfare
Raze	Raise
Foul water	Waterfowl
Fined	Find
Forfeit	Fit for
Outgoings	Going out
Work Life	Life work
Wear away	Away wear
Noose	Nous
Cash in hand	Hand in cash
Beat up	Upbeat
Popery	Potpourri
Go-getting	Get going

Weather Divinations

When a bandicoot scrapes a timber fence with its claws
that is a sign of impending hail. If you walk through a bog

in bare feet and no leeches suck your blood then the sky
will be clear for five days and you can go swimming and hiking.

Fast for three days, lick your finger and if the wind blows
the spittle towards the left the dew will be heavy. If it blows

the spittle to the right then there will be blossom showers,
contrails, and buff-shouldered falcons riding belts of light

winds in the Calms of Capricorn. If a rare blue finch
comes to your window there will be a week of black ice

and sunsets the colour of the head wounds of murdered
seismologists. If a flock of crows sits on your roof

there will be a battle of cold and warm fronts and a volcanic
eruption causing crop failure, landslides, and acid rain.

When a crane sits on the back of a crocodile it means dust
devils will blow. If it sits on the back of a snapping turtle

gales will form causing fishing boats to anchor in narrow
channels where oiled seabirds cry out and drown.

48

If a goat, a ferret, and a rat come to the door there'll be flash
flooding in Africa, a blizzard in the Bahamas, and a beam of light

clearing the fog on Brockenspectre Mountain. If the goat comes
alone the day will be calm, but if it comes walking backwards

with a thorn in its hoof, or accompanied by a goldfinch there'll
be a tornado and a mock sun. If a climate change denier comes

to your door then watch the sky for sheet lightning in towering
banks of cumulonimbus, and go to them with a simoon

on your breath, blood rain in your voice and speak of temperatures
not even the frigate bird sailing through a storm could predict with

its forked tail and puffed chest, nor a line of larks following smoke
from a chimney which is a clear sign of drought, nor the shadow

of a whistling kite falling over fields which is a sure sign of fire—
oh, go to them and grieve knowing they can't read the signs.

Reading the Clouds

Ragged clouds that live at low-level, a lumpen proletariat
unable to rise to the troposphere and take up the anvils of power
*
Clouds that weep because they know climate change will
enlist them in a war where they'll be turned into turrets and
battlements
*
Clouds that want to accompany us like elegant parasols
or that ask us to lie on our backs and watch them shapeshift
into elephants, palominos, camels, steamships
*
Clouds that long to be popcorn, meringue, cotton candy
*
Clouds that long to be cheeses: ricotta, brie, mascarpone, queso fresco,
buffalo mozzarella living together in vast blue larders
*
Clouds that long to drop their Latin names for sweeter ones:
bridal veil, egret wing, water lily, snow goose, arctic swan
*
Clouds that love to follow capricious eddies of air up mountains
where they can watch planes dip and drop and yaw
*
Michelangelo-clouds whose lightning strikes resemble
the finger of God reaching towards Adam
*
Patrician clouds in factory-smoke skies dreaming of the perfumed air
above pines awash with the moon's silver, the sun's gold

50

*

Clouds that long to live underground like truffles

*

Clouds ambitious to be mistaken for UFOs

*

Clouds that dream of visiting the horse latitudes, an all-inclusive
experience of blue skies, privacy, and no wind

*

Agoraphobic clouds staring into tiny windows

*

Clouds that weep because they know they will never have the florid,
expressive ornamentation found on baroque architecture
only the sobriety of Nordic functionalism

*

Clouds that are the thought bubbles of numbskulls and nincompoops
found above the broadcast sites of Fox news

*

Clouds that have had poems written about them and posted
on the Cloud Appreciation Society webpage

*

Clouds that are the wedding dresses of spinster aunts

*

Clouds that look as if they use too much stiffening spray
or have undergone excessive management like Donald Trump's hair

*

Clouds that long to be the bouffant hairdos of Marie Antoinette
Lady Gaga, 90s Madonna, or any drag queen

*

Clouds that mimic Albert Einstein's tonsorial neglect

*

Clouds that love the sound of their droplets hitting the ground
and love it even more when the droplets bounce and hit bystanders
(NB: these clouds can be found mostly in Scotland)

The Walk

To ease a compressed nerve in my back I took a walk,
but soon I wondered if the pain killers had started to trip
nightmare neural circuits because I heard a flock
of lorikeets ballyhooing, and the creek played over stones a tune
from a decrepit piano. I saw eucalypts spark like the electric poles
of dodgem cars, cockatoos spruik from skeletal branches,
crows were opening and closing their wings like flaps
into marquees staging freak theatre, and kookaburras
sent up peals of corrosive laughter when a brush turkey
with a conjoined twin on its back crossed the path to greet
an atavistic specimen of bush rat whose deformities
brought a tear to my eye. Whatever the reason for the bush
turning into a gross floor show, the carnival barkers
kept on. Leaves flashed like cards in the crooked fingers
of fortune tellers, so I walked over a small bridge
to a clearing where a silver frog with a fetish for incandescent
insects sat with its long tongue glittering. I wondered
what menagerie it had escaped from, poor specimens
of biological rarity, and just then, an encephalitic butcherbird
swooped and severed the frog's tongue, swallowing it like a dagger.
I know that pain is a window into the grotesque.
I know the mind can torture with both real and imagined
possession but by then I'd had enough of disablement
and deformity presented as entertainment, worried that next
I'd see a purple echidna forced to swallow flames.
I found my way out by following clumps of orange fairy floss
webbed in trees as if carnival spiders had been hard at work

or Harpo Marx and Lucille Ball had ripped out handfuls
of their hair. As I left the reserve a dwarf pink pademelon
stroked its beard, readjusted its tricorn hat. It was holding
a Harpo Marx doll ventriloquising *Al-A-Ga-Zam*
Al-A-Ga-Zam though the doll's mouth remained firmly shut.
Then it switched phrases: *lama gazal lama gazal*
a near anagram. I yelled back *ptomaine* a near anagram
of pantomime. The pademelon ventriloquised *pharma hoax*—
then *brat trump*, close anagrams of the doll's name
and of PT Barnum. I said *sciatic nerve*—it returned
craven nectaries. Then it yodelled, laughed, put the doll
in its pouch and tunnelled quickly into a patch of long grass.

The Bizarre Bazaar

an homage to Wallace Stevens

What can you buy at the Bizarre Bazaar?
You can buy haar in a jar, blood from an abattoir.
You can buy the hoopla when the pop-singers arrive.
You can buy the oompah of a Bavarian band
and sell it to the cobbler sitting in a chair
spilling oranges and coffee down his pink peignoir.

You can buy the fourteenth way of looking
at a blackbird. You can buy the caftan of Chieftain
Iffucan of Azcan who likes havoc, bruhaha,
likes to tic it, tock it, turn it true to the cha-cha,
the rhumba, the pas de deux and play along
with the man playing things never as they are

on his woeful, woad guitar. You can buy
baklava and nougat, but don't buy the ice cream
it was licked by the emperor's sick chihuahua
when staying at The Palaz of Hoon. You can buy
the parakeet of parakeets, a budgerigar going
ga-ga. You can buy the fracas in an isobar,

a drop of water full of storms, a porcupine's
birth scar, the nothing that is not there, the nothing
that is. You can have tea at The Palace of the Babies
and sing along with the pinewood bantams
and the mother of the babies whose repertoire
is pathos and pity, then talk to the man whose

pharynx is bad, a fustian showman who gives
seminars on snowmen from a wrecked pink sidecar
parked in his grandma's garage. You can buy starlight's
eyesight falling to earth. You can buy the house
of the commissar who burnt down the kasbah—
it's there in his memoir which you can buy at a price

though it's a lot of old hoo-ha, a poem trying to take
the place of a mountain, metaphor as crowbar,
quite the literary faux pas. You can buy the *shoo-wops*
and *doo-dahs* in songs whose lyrics never seem to finish.
You can buy light from a quasar and trade it in for
a shofar and the old song that will not declare itself

despite a vast ventriloquism and the man playing
things not as they are on his woeful, woad guitar.
You can buy the travelogue of thunder, cigar ash
of drunkards, the foppish refinement of the petit
bourgeois, the la-di-da spaces, stairways, and entrances
of the Palace of Versailles. You can buy a fish-scale

sunrise and the moonlight that fubbed the girandoles.
You can buy a statue of the pietà hidden on the peak
of tattered Mt Peckinpah, a mountain covered in cats.
You can buy roses that reign over rows of fine rain,
the floweriest flowers dewed with the dewiest dew.
You can choose what to chew: halvah or caviar,

mints made of mince, trout under sauerkraut,
yolk in an artichoke, peaches covered in sardines.
You can buy knick-knacks nicked from a knackery
like this clavicle from the nabob of bones. You
can buy the band that was banned when it blew
blue notes. You can buy the hackles of a hen

and the enchanted cachinnations of grackles.
You can buy the rights to the Isle of I'll, the crew
of a cruise you'll never take—like that holiday
in reality. You can buy the homilies of Houyhnhnms,
the hankering hymns of the thin men of Haddam
and all the hullaballoo that will make widows wince.

4. Choirwood

Harbour Park at Dusk

All day from the pier to the headland the sky has been
Whiteley blue. Along the shore casuarinas whisper *sassafras
sassafras*—then when the wind changes *susurrus susurrus*.
Soon shadows will barcode the streets, fruit bats fly over
like sheets of carbon paper. There are still some walkers
about, and joggers free of the workday's cinching stricture,
Fitbit their running pace, smart-watch the marathon
vim of their hearts. Boats at anchor tinkle, then settle,
then in the loft and chop from a ferry's wash tattle up
another recital, brief notes from xylophones and toy pianos.
Dogs follow their noses—quick black cursors exploring
menu options. A few children ride bicycles at merriment's
top speed, they ride without the need for finish lines,
only the joy of unbounded revolutions, bright helmets
candy-coat their heads. Now I fix my gaze on an egret
walking where the water holds all the perfections
of a finishing school mirror—it seems to have a piety
born from its sublime indifference to any human presence.
A little girl jumps up and down, giggles as waves pucker
through her toes. She laughs at some pelicans duck-walking
along the sand, a Charlie Chaplin appreciation parade.
A crested hawk that has been riding an air current drops,
hovers—a prayer-crafted cross—small crabs run quickly
like fingers over fretboards practising a funky picking.

The Blowhole

A rumbling—lugubrious as breath blown into a bottle—
     then suddenly a wave pours through the chamber
     and out of the vent
hangs spray in the air—a diamond-studded, up-ended
     wedding dress. Now another one, an unravelling bolt
     of lightly woven shimmer,
higher this time, almost as high as the lighthouse on the hill—

     until gravity tatters it, rips it apart on the rocks.
     A small crowd gathers
waiting for more unfrocking, more allurement of the sea's
     floating attire—but the surface is flat,
     waxen as cerecloth—
no whitecap drapery, no lacy froth, no gauzy blow,
     no confettied mirth. Still the crowd waits for a spill,

     for a spurt, for a view
of wildly exuberant surf. Nothing. No roisterous thunder
     is filling the chamber—the vent's a cloister sealed
     with silence, with an avowed
secrecy of veils. Only the lighthouse commands our viewing—
     immovable, solid, heavy and dressed like a pope
     surveying the abstinent sea.

Estuary

The light is a moving object, an installation
filling the river and the large gallery of the sky—
and if it could be heard as it touches the shallows,
flares along the wavelets and the tips of reeds,
or catches on paperbark leaves, it would be
a singing bowl of seven metals or a set
of water-tuned musical glasses. A family of ducks
float, the young soft and yellow, weightless
as handfuls of wattle blossom. In the distance
a Brahminy kite circles, a piece of kinetic art
turning in the wind. I walk over rocks,
see on the sand shells like broken dinner plates,
herons graceful, stepping with all their weight
on their toes, as if at any moment they might
leap or pirouette. A few crabs slip sidewards
quick as hands playing brisk passages from Liszt
before they bunker down into the gritty
seclusion of their holes. There's a path
I want to reach, one that leads to a look-out,
a headland of coastal banksias whose flowers
are as tough and wiry as the brush-heads
of bottle scrubbers, and from where you
can see the light glimmer on the ocean
which if it were turned into an act of hearing
would be the crescendos, the harmonics,
the note-shaping and evolving timbres, and continuous
pitch blends of a magnetic resonator piano.

At the Lake

I love it here—especially early morning when light
star-tips the leaves, or when a heron drifts, unweighted,
like steam hushed from a teapot's slim spout. The silence
is mixed in with the light, a fine suspension in the lake's

wistful shimmer. Soon I'll reach the rock platform—
the best view of the lake, with coots and little grebes,
reflections of trees ironed onto the water, a sparrowhawk
riding a carousel of air above a stand of melaleucas

with tattered, layered bark—a fringe of botanical grunge
near the tailored limbs of the salmon gums. A small lizard
lies on a rock, shining like a strip of scrap metal. Further
into the bush a brush turkey rakes leaves, a yellow wattle

dangles from its neck—the limp rubber of a burst balloon.
It's a joy to be here at any time of day, no matter
the weather's mood—even if rain veils the lake, or wind
slam-dances in the trees, or moshes the leaves into a wild circle,

or cockatoos screech and the noisy miners act out
militia-punk fandom, diving, clicking their beaks at other birds—
because any moment can impart beauty, like this patch
of mauve flowers, or this dragonfly tie-pinned to a leaf,

glitter-flashes on the water, or this creek running over stones
bubbling, gurgling like a young magpie learning adult songs.
Today wrens are flitting near the bamboo canes packed
densely as organ pipes, their tails flick in time with their quick

jerks and twitches. Gnats are dancing around each other
swapping orbitals like electrons in a subatomic choreodrama.
Suddenly a kingfisher dives into the lake. An egret lowers
a leg into the water the way a scribe might load a brush

with ink, pondering a new script. A few noisy miners
are trying to oust crows from a branch—a separatist clique
endlessly declaring thug rules—the birds don't budge,
they sit like shiny black shoes: ultra-stylish, ultra-supreme.

On a Forest Trail One Sunday Afternoon

Shadows spill towards the creek, rotting leaves smell of peat
and leached tannins. In the trees magpies chortle
then lightly run a line of choriambs across their vocal chords,

preparations choristers might make, bubbling up sounds
before an evening of carolling. Cockatoos add their up-talk
and vocal fry. Further into the scrub a brush turkey

back-kicks leaves onto a mound, then scrapes some away
as if aiming for the steamy ambience of a Turkish bathhouse.
A honeyeater spells its weight around a banksia, swiftly

applying its tongue to the flowers as though it were a tiny
make-up brush. Sugar ants touch feelers, twerking their
abdomens to a beat of bounce music heard only through this

coded exchange. Now the wind gets up—*Sibelius Sibelius*
it seems to say—then *Sisyphus Sisyphus* as it pushes
into the reaches of the blue gums—you'd swear that rushing

was a waterfall's—a white gown cutting loose from a high
hook—corolla whorls, bouquets of splash, drops falling
down the gauzy erasure of a rock face. Near the creek

mosquitoes—black stitches pulled from wounds; their
whine like little, sticky violins; and among the reeds
an egret, cool, a statue in a classical pose, and you stop,

grateful for the way it settles you, the way it makes you
feel both tranquil and exalted before the mosquitoes
perforate your attention again, or a kookaburra with its cackle.

Now the heat has uploaded the cicada's sharp decibels
and you watch the sky for an update on the approaching
storm, thunder circulating like a major newsfeed.

You long for the sound of the creek again, for its small
silver trickle over the pebbles, but you've reached the road,
the heavy bass of traffic combative as a boom box. Later

you'll try to set something down: preserve a scene or two,
a small moment, though everything streamed with change.
Perhaps the egret will be an image that holds, or the creek,

or the wind's sigh, or the fret of mosquitoes around your head.
Perhaps you'll let the day have its simple dissolution
like the storm that's turned down its volume and disappeared.

The Light on Marrin Bay

See this light's unending glisk of spangly
      wicks, micro-sparkles and flickery tinsel twists.
And look at the white swans drifting in—
      they're light and airy as meringue.

A few ducks dive in shadow under the overhang—
      they bob up where the water
is more magnesium flare, more twinkling gloss
      and mineral quiver. A boat

putts by: wash rolls along the shell-and-shingle
      shore—a tintinnabulum, while further off
yachts take the swell and masts conduct a sound
      like plinking xylophones.

Now a breeze pleats the chrome-pink glint
      near the jetty. Jellyfish are a drift
of pearly bulbs, fish are small confections
      wrapped in foil. Soon the sun

will put more silver on its dazzling empire, more
      stacks of coin and crystal jewel
and sparkling leaf—it's not yet six a.m., the day
      barely begun, but the water is spread

with largesse, all the tips of light that phosphoresce,
        all the ferries and their morning stars,
the rowers' oars turning, lifted up, branded
        by daylight's flare. Each ruffle

or surface shirr a flash of bewitchment. The ducks
        dip down again—then rise flicking
decimals of light from their feathers. Next when
        they dive, there are little zodiacs of bubbles.

Peppertree Bay

It's lovely to linger here along the dock,
to watch stingrays glide among the pylons,
to linger here and see the slanted ease
of yachts, to hear their keels lisp, to see
wisps of spray swirl up, to linger along
the shore and see rowers round their oars
in strict rapport with the calls of a cox,
to watch the light shoal and the wash scroll
and wade in shallows like a pale-legged
bird, sand churning lightly in the waves,
terns flying above the peridot green
where water deepens, to watch dogs
on sniffing duty scribble their noses over
pee-encoded messages, and see a child
make bucket sandcastles tasselled
with seaweed, a row of fez hats, and
walk near rocks back to the jetty where
fishermen cast out with a nylon swish,
hoping no line will languish, no hook
snag under rock, to watch jellyfish rise
to the bay's surface like scuba divers'
bubbles, pylons chunky with oyster shells
where a little bird twitters *chin-cher-inchee*
chin-cher-inchee from its nest under the slats,
to feel that the hours have the rocking
emptiness of a long canoe so I can relax
and feel grateful for the confederacies

of luck and circumstance that bring
me here, and today I might spy
a seahorse drifting in the seagrass
with the upright stance of a treble clef,
or the stately flight of black cockatoos,
their cries like the squeaking hinges
of an oak door closing in a draughty church,
to walk near the celadon pale shallows
again where I'll feel my thoughts drift
on an undertow into an expanse where
they almost disappear, and give thanks
again to the profluent music of the waves
and for all the ways that light exalts
the world, for my eyes and brain changing
wavelengths into colour, the pearly
pinks of the shells, the periwinkles' indigo
and mauve, the sky's methylene blue.

West Winds

Here are the fields I roamed as a child,
      fields wild-flowered and manured where stallions grazed
         and goats cropped the seeding tops.
Fields of wheat and oats, rising, falling, the wind oaring
      them hard. Here are the paddocks I crossed
         to watch girls weave

anklets of dandelion and meadow bane while geese flew
      overhead making their own taut skeins.
         This chicory, this plantain, this clover,
this foxtail, this creeping buttercup, this patch of purple
      sheep's sorrel is where I'd run, snatching at stalks
         and stems, trilling sharp notes

to mimic the furious music of horseflies and bees
      swarming over the lush weave of burdock or vetch.
         All summer I roamed—a scheming
locust, a small dynast spending my days where spears
      and sheaths sifted breezes, grasses so thick they hid
         old foes: hares and foxes, snakes and crows.

Many times across those pastures I thought I could hear
      the breathing of ghost-horses, spirit-mares,
         the soft canter of foals—
but it was always just the whisper of wind. Here is the valley
      where small fires burned, sheep on the hill's rise,
         tracts of snow like wayside

flowers. Here are the mountains, dark smalt against
a magenta dusk with pigeons and parrots, flocks
of starlings and their spiralling
upsweeps, their endlessly reconfigured whereabouts—
and the river, too, pitching into the distance
like the tail of a black horse.

Morning, from the Veranda

Booranga Writers' Centre, Wagga Wagga

There's a loose mesh of webs under the railings,
                threads tattered by time and weather,
                        the spiders gone,
but little birds are making kissing noises in the trees.
Fairy wrens' tails are metronomes of fluctuating tempos:
            vivace and *prestissimo*, they twitter constantly
                    as if their voices were trying to keep up
with their rapidly performing tails. Now the call of a crow,
            dry and crumbling, a decrepitating crackle,
                    but magpies sing as if honey
                            coated their throats,
crooners on stage in the trees. Fantails are catching insects
            on the wing. I'm amazed at how they negotiate
                    the twigs and branches
of every tree, never bumping their heads
                    or clipping their wings.
Fairy wrens forage in the grass, steered by their tails,
            upside-down rudders.
            Light jewels the tops of grass blades
and when the breeze blows they twinkle
as if they were still covered in dew. There's a view
                to some hills, deep blue diluting
                        to a lilac haze.
Four kangaroos have come to the fence,
                    they're silent as a mob of granite boulders
            before they lift and bounce up the hill.

A robin bright as a flare, streaks down from a tree
            and catches what it has spotted on the ground.
Everywhere there is movement,
the unending 'doing' of living things driven to survive,
            to perform illimitable stratagems.
    Now the insects switch height and direction,
                their flight almost too quick
for my eye, their neurons and receptors writing a version
            of the world that seems so different from mine,
yet the manoeuvres are the same: to defy death,
        each day a rehearsal for continuance,
                to go on as if tomorrow were real.
Paper wasps scout along the ceiling looking for nest sites.
        A line of ants moves rapidly across the floorboards—
            they're like hyphens accruing
        when you hold down the computer key.
I think of all the transactions, connections
            I'm witnessing, how everything
is acutely alert, so many tiny senses sifting data
        into likelihoods, approximations—
my own brain, too, bringing its version of the world
            into commission.
Between two trees a spider tests a thread, its length
        and tensile strength, her legs and finicky feet
            picking up scents, shifting air—
        then she hangs, microlight, to wait—until vibrations
come like visions: the ardent steps of a mate,
        the jiggly arrival of prey.

Choirwood

The sun has barely put a curved spall of light
above the horizon, yet the kookaburras are already
broadcasting from the trees, and magpies
are opening the day with bubbly, freely given notes.
I walk towards a pocket of bush glad to leave
the shadows of the house. I look up to a fine
crosshatching of twigs in the gums, many full
of webs, some torn, some still iridescent with dew.
I stop to watch a spider restitch part of the cross
it will lie on hour after hour like a martyred apostle.
The light now is loose and yellow like spooned
honey and I've come to sit by the creek and listen
to its little hymns and to give thanks for what
passes before my eyes: a micro-lettering of ants
blurring one edge of a mossy stone, a case moth
caterpillar building a silk ladder along the trunk
of a she-oak to feed on lichen, a silvereye warbling
from a seed-laden banksia cone. I give thanks
too for the forces and interactions running
beneath it all, the flowing, spinning, changing
dynamics, the 'madrigal field' choiring everything
into existence. Now daylight has spent the night's
scattered earnings, except for the moon, a silver dollar
tripling its worth in the creek and in the puddles
of last night's rain. A butcherbird drops one note
after another into the air, making an acoustic mandala,
phrases for its mate to copy before the wind

sweeps the music away. A currawong's song
shapeshifts through its habitat—entanglements
of branches, leafage, twigs, thickets—before
it settles into a high-pitched whistle, a warning
to the channel-billed cuckoo flying overhead. A bee
whirs giddy joy as its wings conduct a shakeout
of pollen in the bottlebrush, and I think about
the intoning, harmonising, buzzing and quavering
I can't hear: the bonding of molecules, pairings
and transfers of particles, electrons and photons
speeding around the globe, quarks popping in
and out of existence, neutrinos zipping through
bodies, asteroids, planets, all the infrasonic
symphonies of the vast and vibrating invisible fields.

Notes

'Listening to Cicadas': the reference to the human protein *titin* is from the website: https://www.digitalspy.com/fun/a444700/longest-word-has-189819-letters-takes-three-hours-to-pronounce.

'The Bizarre Bazaar': approximately 20% of this poem is made up of words adapted from poems by Wallace Stevens: lines 5–6: 'sitting in a chair/spilling oranges and coffee down his pink peignoir' adapted from 'Sunday Morning'; lines 7–8: a reference to 'Thirteen Ways of Looking at a Blackbird'; lines 8–9: 'You can buy the caftan of Chieftain Iffucan of Azcan' from 'Bantams in Pinewoods'; line 10: 'to tic it, tock it/ turn it true' from 'The Man with the Blue Guitar'; lines 12–13: 'playing things never as they are/ on his woeful, woad guitar' adapted from 'The Man with the Blue Guitar'; lines 14–15: a reference to 'The Emperor of Ice-cream'; line 16: 'The Palaz of Hoon' title of a poem; line 17: 'the parakeet of parakeets' from 'The Bird with the Coppery Keen Claws'; line 19: 'a drop of water full of storms' from 'The Bird with the Coppery Keen Claws'; lines 20–21: 'the nothing that is not there, the nothing/ that is' from 'The Snow Man'; line 21: 'The Palace of the Babies' title of a poem; line 22: 'pinewood bantams' from the title 'Bantams in Pinewood'; line 24: 'pathos and pity' from the poem 'Lunar Paraphrase'; lines 24–25: 'The Man Whose Pharynx Was Bad' title of a poem; line 28: 'eyesight falling to earth' from 'No Possum, No Sop, No Taters'; line 31–32: 'a poem trying to take/ the place of a mountain' title of a poem; line 36: 'the old song that will not declare itself' from 'Metaphors of a Magnifico'; line 37: 'vast ventriloquism' from 'Not Ideas about the Thing but the Thing Itself'; lines 42–43: 'a fish-scale sunrise' title of a poem; line 43: 'and the moonlight that fubbed the girandoles' from 'The Ordinary Women'; line 45: 'a mountain covered in cats' the title of a poem; line 47: 'the floweriest flowers dewed with the dewiest dew' from 'The Man on the Dump'; line 52: the 'nabob of bones' from 'Landscape with Boat'; lines 57–58:

'that holiday/ in reality' the title of a poem; line 59: 'hankering hymns' from 'A High-Toned Old Christian Woman'; line 59: 'thin men of Haddam' from 'Thirteen Ways of Looking at a Blackbird'; line 60: 'hullabaloo' and 'will make widows wince' from 'A High-Toned Old Christian Woman'.

'Estuary': the phrase 'the crescendos, the harmonics,/ the note-shaping and evolving timbres, and continuous/ pitch blends' is adapted from an article on the magnetic resonator piano by Andrew McPherson from the website: instrumentslab.org/ research/mrp.html.

'Choirwood': the phrase 'madrigal field' is from Denise Levertov's poem 'Clouds' published in *The Collected Poems of Denise Levertov*, New Directions, New York, 2013.

Acknowledgements

I respectfully acknowledge that these poems were written on Wallumedegal land, and I pay my respects to the elders past, present, and emerging.

I would like to thank Ivor Indyk, Evelyn Juers and the team at Giramondo for supporting my work for many years.

Grateful acknowledgement is also made to the editors of the following anthologies and journals in which many of these poems first appeared: *Australian Book Review, Best of Australian Poems 2021, Best of Australian Poems 2023, Blackbox Manifold* (UK), *Cordite, fourW Anthology,* HEAT, *Island, Love: 2023 ACU Poetry Anthology, Live Encounters: Poetry and Writing, Meanjin, Spiritus* (USA), *The Weekend Australian, Canberra Times, World Poetry.*

The poem 'Choirwood' was commissioned by Judith Nangala Crispin in 2022 for the Judith Wright Regeneration Road Trip.

The poem 'Two Houses' won the ACU Prize for Poetry, 2023. My thanks to the judges Emeritus Professor Margot Hillel and Professor Robert Carver.

My thanks to Kathryn Halliwell and David Gilbey for a residency at Booranga Writers' Centre, Wagga Wagga, where a draft of the poem 'Morning, from the Veranda' was written.

My sincere thanks to members of the pomegranates poetry group for valuable feedback, and to Stephen Edgar for everything.

About the author

Judith Beveridge is the author of seven previous collections of poetry, most recently *Sun Music: New and Selected Poems* which won the 2019 Prime Minister's Literary Award for Poetry. Her other books have won or been shortlisted for major prizes. She has taught poetry in schools and universities and in the public domain and was poetry editor for *Meanjn* from 2005 to 2016. Her poetry has been translated into several languages. She has edited *The Gang of One: Selected Poems* (2018) and co-edited *Contemporary Australian Poetry* (2016) as well as other anthologies. She lives in Sydney.